FAMILIAR

MONSTERS

of the FLOOD

FAMILIAR

MONSTERS

of the FLOOD

Tia McLennan

Riddle Fence Debuts
St. John's, NL

Riddle Fence Publishing Inc.
PO Box 7092
St. John's, NL A1E 3Y3, Canada
www.riddlefence.com

The publisher gratefully acknowledges the support of the Canada Council for the Arts,
the Newfoundland and Labrador Arts Council, and the Government of NL.

Riddle Fence Publishing acknowledges the land on which we work as the ancestral
homelands of the Beothuk, whose culture has now been erased forever. We also
acknowledge the island of Ktaqmkuk (Newfoundland) as the unceded, traditional
territory of the Beothuk and the Mi'kmaq. And we acknowledge Labrador as the
traditional and ancestral homelands of the Innu of Nitassinan, the Inuit of Nunatsiavut,
and the Inuit of NunatuKavut.

Cover and text design by: Graham Blair
Cover art by: Toni Hamel "The Migration"
Edited by: Adèle Barclay

Printed and bound in Canada

Library and Archives Canada Cataloguing in Publication
Title: Familiar monsters of the flood / Tia McLennan.
Names: McLennan, Tia, author.
Description: Poems.
Identifiers: Canadiana (print) 20230590594 | Canadiana (ebook) 20230590632 |
ISBN 9781738151547 (softcover) | ISBN 9781738151554 (EPUB)
Subjects: LCGFT: Poetry.
Classification: LCC PS8625.L4538 F36 2024 | DDC C811/.6—dc23

For my father, Robbie McLennan, and for my family.

Hold on, nightingale!
Out of the depths it's growing—
we are in disguise.

— Tomas Tranströmer

Contents

Part One

Minimal amount

of free fluid within

pelvis. No evidence

of a live intrauterine

gestation. Close

surveillance of beta

ensure resolution

to normal.

Time in fixative: 04:30.

Fixation duration:

Approximately 72 hours.

Specimen received

in formalin

consists of 4 g

of soft red–brown

tissue. Chorionic

villi are not

definitively identified.

Messenger

An invitation—perfect
cursive, roosts in my
screen's glow. Early spring
is all filth: exhaust
grit-crusted snow banks draw
back, lay bare last season's garbage,
dog shit. Signs of life:
a bill paid, numbers vanish reappear,
spears of crocus,
copious tiny, dull feathers slicked
to the sidewalk,
cat's first kill.
Snow and blowing snow—
winter radio report still plays
in my head. Ellipses of long-range forecasts.
I click *Attending*.

Party Trick

The table is an old horse
whose creaks butter our
conversation. She bears
our food, goes nowhere.
Upon her back, a loose symmetry
of white dessert plates with
blackberry smears, glossy
pastry crumbs.

Outside, beyond the imaginary
light of our thoughts, garden
soil shifts with worms'
work. Guests drift
down the front steps, lungs
fill with cool musk of leaf mulch.
Cars turn on, engines tunnel
the saturated dark. The moon
holds water in her open throat.

Ventriloquism

My head is an un-rung bell. My eyes, mouth
arid. The bedroom's air slumps in post-rain humidity.

Anonymous sorrows multiply, shuttle through
my blood. My body archives them in my marrow,

they burrow in my medulla, infiltrate signals to the heart
and lungs. I am open to negotiation.

They call my father; he comes reluctantly
and stands at the foot of my bed. The full moon

turns the world outside into a B-movie set. The director barks
Action! Actors tilt their faces towards the cool light,

play drunk. Cue the coyotes. Their voices lifted by thin, taut
silver wires. I try to throw my own voice toward a future self.

But miss. I've been running a tab too long. The moon
herself is broke. *I can't run this place on thin air*

you know. The bell is rung with force, but now this is
a silent movie projected on silver screen. One last look

at my father before I wake. In his muted face,
I see the unmistakable shape of my mouth.

Honeybark

When we were children
I had a funny idea: what if
we were on an airplane and
our happiness was the only

thing that kept the plane aloft?
Imagine a sad passenger:
we must cheer them up!
We acted it out, laughed until

we cried. We made our own
economy, traded almost anything.
The most valued currency
we named Honeybark:

translucent, hard, golden-amber
globs picked like scabs from
the trunk of the old cherry tree.
We lined windowsills with our riches.

We sucked sugar-dipped, pink-green
rhubarb stalks. We wore on our mothers'
nerves, wore the cherry tree's low, thick
branches down to a shine. One day,

my friend silently fell backward off the edge
of the treehouse. The next day we swarmed
her new leg cast with markers. A multitude
of suns, balloons, crooked rainbows adorning
the cool hard white canvas of *what if*

Examination

Height 171 cm.   *weight 69 kg.*

He is in no acute distress. He is not jaundiced.

> Hair and dust gathered from the floor,
> the fan hums, churns the heat, wait
> for the oncologist's call from across

Head and neck exam is unremarkable.

> the Pacific. One translation of
> yoroshiku onegaishimasu is
> *please, treat me with kindness.*

His oropharynx is clear.

> Through the far end of a drainpipe,
> an unreachable paradise.

Cardiovascular exam reveals normal heart
sounds with no additional murmurs or rubs.

> Train schedule's Kanji
> remains abstract

He lives in Garden Bay, on his own.
His daughter lives in Japan, but
she is planning to return.

> art. Predicted rain
> arrives heavy,
> at a slant.

Making Money from Home

Awake with the erratic siren;
a coyote weaving the valley

chants code: three yips, a howl.
Pause. Looped. The moon floods

the frozen landscape. The coyote's
voice stitches together our careful,

private distances. So close at one point,
she seems just below my window,

calling up. Calling on all the corroded
things I work to forget. Come morning,

the ferries are fucked up again.
Someone's hacked my email,

telling all my contacts how they can
make money from home. At night

the rain sounds uncertain, falling
heavily then barely falling.

Wishbone

Left to dry on the ledge above
the stove. Once hidden
where chest met neck,
now a dry, uncertain
talisman in our rented
kitchen.

My mother and I
would each hook our baby
fingers around the bone's arc,
pull until the *snap*
allowed one of us a wish.

What year did I choose to be
a ghost? Drizzle weighed
down the white sheet, cut-out
eyes kept shifting. The plastic
pumpkin grew heavy
with the kindness
of strangers.

Easter in Arizona.
A girl wanders into
the desert and the desert
rises up to meet her. She
searches for eggs her parents
have hidden. Now the sun
rises, colouring the world

as if she's inside a tangerine,
looking out. The family heads
south. The sun climbs to its apex.
Some eggs remain hidden
under scrub brush, cacti.
They shimmer, and soften
beneath thin foil.

Daughter Takes Inventory

A postcard to an aunt
from the travelling young man,
asking for a little money.

Photos peeled from
yellowed pages
of albums.

The small woven basket on the dresser—
lifting its lid: brass bullets,
someone's war medals.

A heavy old tin full
of lost keys.

An emergency supply
of liquid morphine.

The plastic syringe by the bathroom sink
caked in fine white crystal dust,
hair on a brown plastic brush.

A brown plastic brush, a framed poster
of Einstein: *I want to know
God's thoughts. . .*

The feeding machine,
its clear tubes dangling
beside the stripped bed.

An old .30-30 Winchester rifle—
trigger-locked, hidden—
without a license.

Souvenir

I dreamt I was felling
dead alders around the yard
—silver-grey bark coming
easily away from their trunks
into my hands at the faintest
suggestion—the night before
I woke early, unwrapped
the plastic wand, held it beneath
me and carefully peed. Chemistry
is also why he and I fell together
for a quick fuck in the West End apartment
he was house-sitting. When we
came, our bodies seemed to lift
right off someone else's bed.
My decision sinks like a quarter
tossed off the end of Davis Bay Pier.
It spins deeper through winter-clear
water, growing smaller, glinting.
Now the technician slowly moves
the wand inside my body, her monitor
translates sound to image. *It's still
very early.* She points to the dark
oval blob and for a moment I am
looking through a telescope, observing
a black hole, or a starless corner
of the universe. *I can't even tell
if there's anything alive in there.*

Gumboots

I had meant to take them
to the thrift store but kept
forgetting, so they
stayed: one under
the cover of the portico,
the other's mouth open
to early spring rain
until brimming, it bulged.
For days, I stepped
out the door, struck
by the sense that someone,
in a rush, had left part
of their leg behind.
The boot made an oval
frame, a portrait clutched
by the water's surface:
climbing honeysuckle—
in new leaf
against the sky.

Perigee

I was pulling
a red wagon up the hill,
toward the house.
In the wagon sat my dad,
holding a glass of wine.
Slosh. We were nearly there,
but I couldn't pull anymore.
*Dad, you have to get out
and walk.* He did, his legs
wobbling like a brand-new colt.
My cat appeared,
limping in my direction.
In his paw a gaping hole—tiny
parasitic bugs were burrowing.
I tried to kill them, sliced
them in two with the sharp
crescent of my thumbnail.
But this only caused them
to multiply, each half
born anew.

Undertaker

No sign, just a small brick
building. I ring the doorbell, a slight
man answers. His *hello* has no greeting.
He wears an argyle sweater. I say my father's
name. He gestures and I follow
through the narrow, carpeted hallway
to some hard-backed chairs where I must
wait. His sweater disappears around
a corner, and I'm left facing a heavy red
curtain—but there's a gap. Between
curtain and wall, I see a white-socked
ankle and the grey pant cuff of a man
who's no longer his body. The undertaker
returns, snaps the curtain closed, keeping
the living from the dead. He holds out
a small white box with my father's name
typed on the label. I need both hands. I thank him,
then hear my voice ask, *How hot does it get
to bring a body to ash?* When he speaks,
he looks past me. On the drive home
I try to remember his answer.

Event Horizon

I give my arm. Blue mask
and kind eyes, he taps my vein
to call it to my skin's surface,
slides the needle into the site.
Liquid bends through the clear
tube toward me until: dim
smell of strawberry milk,
a dream of a man, once family,
I no longer speak to. Astronomers
try to pinpoint rapid radio bursts
from a faint galaxy, turn the house
upside down, searching for dark
matter, make the world into an
earth-sized lens that will capture
an image of a black hole's edge. I
come to. My body retches to rid
itself of unnatural sleep. My
anesthesiologist's gone, taken
gentle hold of someone else's arm
in the metallic theatre. Lights bear
down, eradicating shadow. While
I fumble delirious behind thin curtains,
in a standard issue, pale blue gown
to get my socks on, he tells them
now count backwards from ten.

The Old Island Highway

More than seven thousand kilometers away
on the jagged eastern edge of this country,

if I squint, I can see my virginity. Like any
mythical creature, it could only claim its

existence once it was lost. Lured by the
highway's velocity, it thumbs south, walking

the gritty shoulder backward between
ditch and going somewhere, following

our long, elastic shadows, the drone of cars.
A beacon of brake lights. Drifting up through

the rolled down window: *Where you girls
headed?* Now, far from girlhood, they slip out

of the dark rooms where their children sleep.
Sometimes the mothers' thoughts flicker toward

each other. Steps are retraced. Flesh, cells, nerves
house uneasy coalitions. Close calls harboured

at the bases of their spines. In their spare
time, they work furiously to decode

their bodies' intelligence. If only to reveal
what is genetic, what is taught.

Hungry

Driving around the gravel bend
in Dream Valley and catching
a slim coyote gliding down
the middle of the road toward
me. I slowed, hoping to get a closer
look at something wild. It veered
off, refusing my predictable need
to know. I was returning from
the clinic where the dentist
ground down one of my
canines. Made my bite
nearly perfect.

Chimera

She is having trouble remembering her childhood so she
researches her family tree. With two heads (three if you count
the snake—but the snake's busy keeping watch for the men
who are always trying to kill her), she can read twice as fast.
She knows now about her maternal grandparents. Ceto—
goddess of the dangers of the sea, of sea monsters, whales,
giant sharks—consorted with her brother Phorcys (incest is
nbd when you're a primordial god).

It is written that the only reason Zeus let Ceto's mother
Echidna live was because he needed her to produce monsters
that could be killed to make heroes out of men. Zeus banished
her, along with her lover Typhon (the serpentine god of storms
and volcanoes), to a cave beneath a mountain. Typhon had
had the nerve to try and overthrow Zeus's rule of the cosmos.
This was how Zeus dealt with revolutionaries. And they stayed
in the cold, wet dark of a cave, occasionally sneaking out to
feed on unsuspecting travellers. So the story goes. And this is
where Chimera and her siblings were born.

Her memories of the cave are vague. She doesn't remember any details of her siblings. She didn't get to grow up around them. But she lets herself imagine that early, loving chaos—so many young monsters echoing in the cavern, climbing over their exhausted parents. In that dark home she imagines, briefly, they were a family. Then a man named Amisodorus, a king from Lycia, came for her—she doesn't remember this moment either. He raised her, made sure she became full monster, first by befriending her, then teaching her cruelty and rage. He set her loose.

The Chimera has heard rumours of another possible self: one who was a fierce protector, revered for fertility and strength, whose rage and fire-breath was fueled by love, like a mother's love. She knew being a mother wasn't for her, knew one day a man would finally end her, that his victory would be celebrated—perhaps even long after he was dead—while her story would be taken, passed down as *monster* through the mouths of one hero after another.

Part Two

Findings:

Previously noted

gestational sac

yolk sac and tiny

embryonic pole

no longer

identified.

Options for management.

Surgical risks and complications:

bleeding, transfusion, infection,

uterine perforation and its

sequelae, visceral

injury, need for laparoscopy

or laparotomy. She fully

understood the risks.

She elected to

proceed.

Predictions

A plane full of passengers has
gone missing. With the daylight,
the search for the black box resumes.

By February 2015, we could all be
making purchases with our heartbeats.

Hands reach through the plastic tubing
on either side, they both extend one finger,
the baby's walnut-sized fists open.

Out my window the snowed yard
grows bluer, dimmer.

The doctor:

Some babies make it, some don't.

Your timeline is interrupted
with a gift:

All the minted minutes you waited.

Plenty of Fish

She returns from circling
the day, falls into
the cool blue light, scrolls
through faces. Under
hobbies and interests

MountainMan has written
stargazing, way-finding.
But starlight is so old, why
navigate by burning referents
that may not even exist?

The house is dark. Night,
a welcome stray, comes
close, crouches, laps
a little milk from the
shallow bowl. Humming

of the fridge slips into her
dream. Lost in a field of grain
up to her forehead. At the crack
of dawn, they turn on the
machines for the harvest.

Ash Wednesday

Did you depart under
the new moon's clean
black slate? Mostly
ghost, tinkering with form,

you remained before that
threshold, couldn't cross
over. Maybe it was the day
I stopped

at the grocery store to buy
a half-priced Valentine's
bouquet? On the kitchen
counter, I laid them in a bar

of late winter light. I divided
flowers, red from white. Found
the smallest vases and placed
them in separate rooms.

Revision Notes

I have the feeling you could keep going.
Scene break in the second line,
a moment of waking.

"Brighter-than-day"—rework
as in metallic Walt Whitman:
"When I Heard the Learned Astronomer"

Event Horizon/Black Magic liquid
move second stanza—disrupt
syntax, more disorientation

Revise this so you're in the silence
between the initial pattern
of beeps.

How the "you" of the poem
is at the mercy of the
narrative voice

Cut out "and" for more ambiguity.
Cut out "Event Horizon"
Cut out "disoriented"

(Show don't tell—more space
imagery) "Another woman's
arm?" Either double down

or back off on "woman"
I suggested you delete
"ever." Tie this subtly to

the time signal. Wilderness
haunted by faint contours.
End: bring us outside again.

A found poem assembled from the gracious and insightful
feedback I received from poetry mentors and editors Adèle
Barclay, Leah Horlick, and Mark Callanan. My deepest
thanks.

Now You Have Full Access

I have updated your address
and added your darkest thoughts to the file.

You must fill out the forms
using only spit and moonlight.

If you forget your password,
press your face to the earth in springtime.

If you cannot recover it,
try lying in a dim room,
imagine the ocean on a calm day,
or call the number at the bottom

of the screen. Though be advised: due to
high tides, wait times are longer than normal.

Your code will expire tomorrow at midnight,
dissolving into a heavy dew
that will briefly silver morning.

If the light is right

If you are there to see it

Making Stock

Simmer all day until
bones soften, onion
surrenders translucent.
As it cools, the surface
will gleam: tiny, perfect
circles of grease. Let gristle
float to the top. Shallow
scoop skimmed off
the moon. You can use
layered cheesecloth.
Are you different?
Strain. Clarify. Now
ready for the freezer:
a row of yogurt containers
filled to a finger below
their rims. Double-wrap
remnants in plastic,
freeze until the next
garbage day.
If you have
trouble falling asleep,
try cutting your hair,
let soft, dark commas
fall, overlap, into the
bathroom sink.
If you still can't sleep,
play a recording of frog songs,
use a warm face cloth,
give yourself a temporary
name. Did you forget
the tilt of the earth?
This amphibious moon
submerges animate
and inanimate alike.

Missing No One

Yesterday made six years
of my father's absence. I walk
to meet an old lover at
an affordable hotel in
the city and we make love
out of habit. Daylight, a solvent,
thins everything: twisted
sheets, orange peels afloat
in the silver ice bucket. We
say goodbye, find our own
ways home. Nights later,
missing no one, I bake apple
crisp. Pick up Milosz's *Bells
in Winter*, accidentally smear
cinnamon on a page, try to
rub it off. When sleep comes,
a smooth, black stone floats
up from my chest, rests
on my tongue, provides
the cool weight of relief. I have
nothing to say.

From A War

The old curved sword that hangs
above the bedroom door
has been in the family since when?
From a war no one living can
name or place.

Dragnets of rain tilt
from the coast mountains,
sweep over our house, ghost
out toward open Pacific,
leave nothing behind.

Behind the beaded curtain,
my mother is practising. She twirls,
drops her veil, shimmies her belt of coins.
Soon she'll take me; we'll be gone.
My grandmother never trusted

her daughter-in-law. My last visit
to her hospital bed, her thin hands
light as birds. She asked me for an ice cube,
it slipped from the paper cup
into her mouth.

Nurses' muted words, flick
of their wrists closing curtains to
the day. She became a paper
lantern, shedding light on
nothing in particular.

My Twelfth Summer

We made pickles in a borrowed house.
I had no room and slept on a flower-print

sofa, air heavy with vinegar and dill.
The scent wove itself into my long, dark hair.

I woke to the stillness of the house.
Pop-ting—another jar sealing, a

nauseous pain clung to my center,
pulled me down towards the earth

like a dumbbell. Dark smear on
my inner thighs. I understood

but had been expecting cardinal red.
Like the time I was six, naked in

the shallows of a silty northern river,
whipped a stick at an older boy who'd

splashed me, and saw his hands fly
to his forehead, bright red seeped

through his fingers. They took him
away in the back of a pickup to get stitches.

I ran into the tall dry river reeds,
thinking *From now on, I must live*

alone. But that night it was old blood I saw,
my body having quietly rearranged itself.

I lay anchored on the sofa. Mesh of dill
and brine in my lungs, sea of cricket song

lapping at the window's screen and
from the predawn kitchen, jars lined up,

packed to just below their rims,
a chorus of popping.

Doppler Interrogation

Technician's finger on the mouse.
A series of clicks.
Cold, clear, gel-slick.
The monitor's dim green light
on the slight rise of my belly

looks like an alien landscape.
Echolocation. There
are no bearings.
The technician fills in
all the blank fields. Routine

naming, numbering,
the unknown. Thin white
towel to wipe off the gel.
Lights shiver on. Day
commutes to night.

Mistaken Point

At first glance they seemed
perfect; frozen in mid-flight.
Beneath overlapped clouds—
shrinking in layers toward
horizon. Parched light
on water. We came

to Mistaken Point to run our
fingers over 565-million-year-old
fossils. To try to fathom deep time,
to see if our own far-flung
existence could muster relief
in something smaller and

vaster than ourselves. We looked
up from the base of the white pillar:
the metal lantern of Cape Race's
lighthouse. The giant glass optic
spun. Come darkness, it will
broadcast its light. Who

should receive it? We counted
nearly thirty, surprised by the
varied species. All face down
in thick grass, wings outstretched
or folded neatly. Storm petrels,
sooty shearwaters, whimbrels,

common murres, black-legged
kittiwakes. Feathers undisturbed,
evenly spaced, like someone had
fastened them to an invisible grid.
Dumb, unable to read this signal,
we walked back to the gift shop,

the cashier on her break leaning
against the clapboard facade,
loosely holding her cigarette. She
shrugged, *Sometimes it
happens, not sure why.* Wind
pulled smoke straight up

like yarn from the corner
of her mouth as if drawing
out a trespassing spirit.
Cold gusts stole our talk,
ushered us toward our car.
I didn't know I was pregnant.

Reconnaissance

A curled, palm-sized photo of
Grandpa: wearing white socks,
open black cardigan. He rests
in the half-constructed garden,
leaning back on the rock wall,
legs outstretched. With photo

in hand, I walk uphill toward the
house on Duchess Avenue, take
the alley. Striated clouds against
blue linoleum sky—waves of
spilt milk. Open the back gate,

pocket the photo, wade through
thigh-high grass, past the place
where once I cupped a small,
stunned bird in my hand. The cat
watched angrily. For a long time,

no one moved. Evening swallowed
day. Without a sign, the bird
was gone. It's important not to get
distracted. Walk through the back
door as if you are ten. You will find

Yorkshire puddings rising in the oven
—little clouds at dawn, blue collector
plates commemorating the provinces
still surround the dining room
walls. But you aren't ten.

The hazel tree was cut down,
then the rare magnolia. The deck
softened, garden turned loose.
Photos of Grandpa long packed away.
Return to this point: Grandma rests

in the TV light, on the couch,
her head slouched to the side, mouth
parted in sleep. Slim fingers prop
a smouldering cigarette. Relax, let
go. She will wake up when the room

fills with smoke. Her son will make
a phone call. Soon she will leave
this house for good, for a nowhere
of curtains, white walls, nurses,
meals in small portioned cups.

No more cigarettes. Time has spasmed
another future. You return, but there is
no record; you don't know the place where
she is buried. Bowed photo, cupped palm.
No sign or movement.

Night Dive

A moonless November
night, neoprened bodies
of our diving class take turns
stepping off the rain-swollen
dock into the motionless bay.
Caught in beams of our lights:
sun and starfish, sea anemone,
a startled octopus whose ink
briefly billows us into complete
darkness. Sound of regulators,
exhaled bubbles. Minutes. The ink
dissipates, we use hand signals
to say *I'm ok* and *Let's ascend.*

*

A decade later, I will listen
to the radio all through January,
to hear *Assiniboine* and *Red River*
—the names themselves a kind
of flooding. Somewhere in the
basement, packed away, a small
glass box that holds my wisdom
teeth. I tell my father I have
a gift for him, but it's not ready
yet. If the house could speak,
it would say it's happiest in
the rain. Where roof meets
the uncontrollable sky,
sustained applause.

Bivalve

I google *mussels,*
looking for a video
of undulating pale
tasselled gills that siphon
water just beyond the
parted black razor edge
of shell. I want to put
this description
in a poem. Instead, I find:

> *A Billion Seashore Animals*
> *Cooked Alive During*
> *Pacific Northwest Heat Wave.*

Apparently, the smell hovered for days,
rising under the Vancouver harbour
heat dome. The next video in my search
demonstrates how mussels are an excellent
measure for microplastics. I watch

a biologist hold a tiny blade, deftly slice
open the supple, dark green liver to obtain
a sample, count parts
per million.

Working the mussel bar station
at the fine dining restaurant
in my twenties, I wore all black
with a rusty-red lipstick.
Made $12.50 plus tips. Alive, alive-o!
Salt, steam, sometimes a man
would joke, *Show me your muscles!*
as I scooped gaping black shells
onto his white plate, and he'd
laugh, and I'd laugh too, and
tell him he wasn't the first
to make that joke.

Deliquescence

VERB (intransitive)

1.*(especially of certain salts) to dissolve
    gradually in water absorbed from the air*
2.*(especially of certain fungi) to dissolve into
    liquid, especially at maturity*
3.*(of a plant stem) to form many branches*

—*Collin's Dictionary*

The doctor draws little figurines
of chromosomes. My pen bleeds,
I throw it in the trash.

Full moon over the ponds, fish
mouth their way to the glow
at the surface. Blood

is drawn every three days,
a new bruise in the crook
of my elbow. Surprised

by comfort in the familiar
sharp smell of cool alcohol
wipes, the sting.

follicles

induration

analgesic

palpate

Winter arrives, our lips
grow chapped. It hurts
to smile. The salt-grey roads'

old asphalt skin breaks into
pot holes. Unintentional ghosts:
plastic bags caught in bare

branches, ribboned by wind.
No one gets their ladder
to untangle them.

My anesthesiologist meets
my eyes. His eyes say nothing.
He is focussed, watching.

I am close to going under.
A fog horn vibrates
against my rib cage.

Gentle sharp curettage.

Empty

instrument count

correct.

Patient returned to

the supine.

The fog still hangs. In the cul-de-sac, fishing
nets collapsed at the mouth of each
driveway; the garbage has been collected.

Confidentiality

Over the grey cubicles, framed
by the towering window, a tugboat glides
through the harbour's open aperture toward

the dark band of ocean at the horizon.
Yesterday the sea was staccato with whitecaps
—animated incisions. The frozen air and sun

chiselling distant details into precise
focus. Today the ocean is unending layers
of matte blue-greys. Distances remain

nebulous. The caller tells me their child
has taken their own life. She tells me
the story. *I'm sorry, I'm so, so sorry.*

For a few breaths it seems she and I are
adrift, horizonless. I process her request. All day,
a small, brass egg, cold and heavy in my belly.

In my dream again, I forget my baby somewhere,
board a plane to retrieve some important papers,
but the plane takes off, takes us far away from

where we need to be. Awake, everything seems
the same. All day the news heading reads:
The Ottawa River Poised to Peak.

Recurring Dream

This time the teeth were
old, hollow, cracked,
the colour of dried grass.
First, they loosened:
one, then, helplessly,
others. I spat them
into my cupped hands
until they were almost
overflowing, found
a container for them.
From the ringing sound
of teeth being poured
into it, I'm pretty sure
it was a glass jar.

The Sixth Miscarriage

transabdominal
endovaginal

echogenic

imaging
aberrations

i.

Turning toward a super
moon. Leonard Cohen
died. Again, rats
in our walls. Cat crouches,
transfixed. Again, we ascend
through the midnight zone
of this north Atlantic winter,
light slowly slides into our
days until the fulcrum
moment it begins to slip.

anterior lip
of cervix

was grasped

with a single
tooth
tenaculum

ii.

The house crooked,
art on walls askew.
My body jolts in sleep,
micro-tremors. Thumb-sized
white squid swim in a black
plastic tub. I google endless
recipes: grilled, sautéed, steamed
fried. I can't decide how
best to kill them.

banded metaphases
hyper   echoic

double decidual
sign

iii.

In finance news headlines:
Animal Spirits Are Running
Away with the Economy.
Bearing bad news clenched
in my teeth, bearing all the
correct forms filled in
black ink. *Bear right,* says
the British female voice of
our GPS, *take the motorway.*

gentle sharp
curettage

the cavity
was felt

to be
empty

iv.

Here is our petri dish
in full bloom, here,
our desire to make
a home. A list
of unused names.
How to rid
the house of dead
rat smell? How to locate
and label a failure
in the flesh? Waves
pass through my film
of skin, nerves, blood
to my bone. Shed light.
But the full moon
is not an X-ray.

necrotic and inflamed

fragments

ghost outlines

of decidua

v.

No one knows why
I'm failing. Laminate
losses. I screenshot
Pinterest plans to build
my own modern furniture
from plywood. Of course
I didn't follow through.
After blood is drawn, I take
my body back to our temporary
home to dwell in the cellular
dream of another body.

instrument and sponge
count was correct

patient was
returned

to the
supine

vi.

New moon, my body rids itself
of everyone's well-meaning advice,
prepares itself for
the wisdom of self-sabotaged
opportunities. To have
poorly diversified.
To have poorly
differentiated. I turn
all the plants
so they do not bend
too far toward the light.

Part Three

Consent obtained.

Patient prepped and draped

in the usual fashion.

dorsal lithotomy

IV sedation

Bimanual

examination revealed

soft, mobile

somewhat boggy

6–8 week-sized uterus.

20 units of oxytocin

in one litre of crystalline.

Microchimeratic

She is becoming many. In a sterile room
white coats count: heads, tails, wraths.

Counting on her to be reducible.
But multilineage cells know how

to differentiate. All the born and
unborn children find refuge in her

body, get to work. Grafted. Chimera:
beast with heads of a lion, a goat, the tail

of a snake. Fire-breathing female. Belly
to the earth. Fluent rage. *Micro* as in *tiny*,

invisible to whose naked eye? Something
living is given to this myth. She splits like

a ripe plum after heavy rain. Her blood
turns polluted; she is admitted. The doctors

won't admit they cannot control the
landscape of her body. It does not stay

together the way they want. Alternate
wrists, try to make it easy for the nurses.

Even science cannot track the new cells' ways
of thinking. And by thinking, I mean following

their ever-evolving blueprint. Her son continues
to crash into her. She cannot remember all

the words to the bedtime songs. When
rage finds her, it locates the weakest

point, a fissure in her surface. She herself
is swallowed, she monsters the familiar.

Ultrasound

Haloed, unfinished
form, the sound of his
work-in-progress body
rendered into light and
dark. Double decidual,
double profile tracing
a slight movement,
ghost-like, unsanctioned

view. Phew. Proof of
normal heartbeat and
measurements. While beyond
these walls an almighty polar vortex
drags the island of Ktaqmkuk
and all her inhabitants further
toward the vanishing horizon
of the open ocean.

Scar Tissue

In the rental on Parade Street, the backyard weeds climb over
and over each other—goutweed, chickweed, the occasional head
of red clover, thigh-high thistles, morning glory and the burnt-red
shoots of knotweed pushing through the unchecked green clamber.
We have ceded the backyard. It has become habitat and we, uncertain
intruders. The day is a cool, wet relief—no need to leave the house.
The baby sleeps. A spindly moment to scribble down signals from
my flesh: constant thirst, hum of new nerve endings. Cell by cell, sleep
by sleep, my body repairs. Pain signals. My thirteen-month-old son cannot
yet understand the dangers of this world. He thinks with his body.
And my body is still his. At night he curls into me, taking an inner form.
The baby sleeps. Now I have enough time to catch the spiders
in the kitchen sink, release them out back, into this lick of near-
wilderness. Meeting the ground, their legs don't hesitate.

Year of the Rat

My husband and son
sleep into the Lunar
New Year. As advised,
I cleaned the night
before so good luck
can arrive, take up

residence undisturbed
by domestic labour.
Is today tomorrow?
my son asks. *Yes,*
yesterday, today
was tomorrow.

The snow that fell
is covered by
a new thin snow.
Wind snakes it
across the empty
street.

If I'm honest,
the house is only
half clean.
We aren't
even married. One
night, when the moon

was waxing gibbous,
my son pointed out
the car window:
The moon is an egg!
While we sleep,
he will leave

his room for ours, mold
his body to mine so
our breaths sync up.
Sometimes, in sleep,
he sucks gently at
air, as if he's

working to get his
fill of dream milk.
The first swallows
are always the fattiest,
feeding cells that
never stop to rest.

A Dream of Misplacing the Baby

I retrace my steps,
heartbeats—small collisions.
Morning comes dandelion-bright
and bitter. It's the sixteenth day the orca
named Tahlequah grieves her calf.
Over and over she holds him

against her forehead, her back, so his
body breaks the surface of the Salish Sea,
into the vital air and the world's
electronic eye. I can't look so I run
errands, do online banking, keep
the baby fed, the kitchen clean.

In the black and white
of the monitor, his chest rises
and falls—ache of watching him
sleep. He has packed on all
the necessary fat. Far west,
in the city of my birth, the sun

appears the colour of salmon roe,
suspended in smoke. We wonder if
we can return. Now, summer thins.
Fat, slow flies weave through the house;
helplessly pulled to daylight,
they buzz furiously against the glass.

Apogee

My father said in last night's
dream he had broken down,
sobbing, the house a mess,
things to get rid of everywhere.

I ask what had made
him cry. It was a torn red
rubber mat. I had a shed
and in it everything was clean,

perfectly organized. He was
going to throw out the mat,
I yelled at him not to. He went
to put it in my shed. I became

enraged. *Just leave it on that rock!*
as if he should know better.
He says it was then he began
crying and couldn't stop.

Late Letter to Dad

Time pours. It remains
undisturbed by rules: seconds,
minutes, grids of days, years.

To think of leaving
as if it were a train station
to move through and we are
always late.

You were hopeful. Those bronzed arms
worked the garden. Now sickness
makes you a stranger

in your own living room. I draw back
my arm and throw. The stick
breaks the perfect
surface of the lake.

The dog swims for it, as she always does.
How could I have guessed
she'd outlive you.

New Regime

The hygienist points to dark
gaps on the X-ray where bone
used to be. *Stress often leads to gum
inflammation. You might be
tender for days.* She brings me
handfuls of trial-sized toothpaste.

At home, I hold warm saline
in my mouth, count to sixty, spit.
I empty my purse, gather the little white
tubes from their boxes, move to put
them in the drawer,
when they slip—

leaping away from me in all directions,
so many small, bright fish.

Radiation

We must reach for our jackets,
another summer slipped through our fingers.

At night, my father calls me out to the deck.
He motions to the sky with his cigarette.

> Three broad arrows of Canada Geese flap south
> against September's star map. So high, their
> calls barely reach us.

In the morning I find him on the deck again,
standing, his back to me, as the morning mist merges

with his smoke. One last one. Leaves unhinge
as we drive, spinning over us,

all the way to St. Mary's and back.
This confetti, this sun.

Swarm

No fixed address, dragging
the weight of fragmented
family history stashed
in Rubbermaids. Is it lying
to straighten your hair

when naturally curly? I cry
wolf all night, remembering
my eighteenth summer:
pollen-smeared, smelling of
fermented propolis, honey.

A beekeeper's assistant, I slept
in a small school bus on blocks
in a sea of grass, dropped acid
with the Deadheads on weekends.
Fireweed season: we moved

sealed hives at night. A leak
in one super—the worker shot
straight at my eye, incapable
of thought for itself. My co-worker
held a flashlight in her mouth,

used tweezers to extract
the stinger, but the venom sac
had pulsed its poison-medicine.
Morning revealed a rainbow bruise
over my swollen-shut eye.

Once we were sold the luxury of
unwinding summer days, drawn
to the pink want of cotton candy, to
the collective silence as the coaster crests
then plummets. Our screams unfurled

above us. Now we know better. I hold
my breath through ten seconds of radio
silence—the National Research Council's
time signal. At the beginning of the long dash
my mind reaches back to the morning
the bees swarmed. The sound of a low-
flying plane. We became fastened
to the earth. They settled—a drooping
form over a low cedar bough. Approaching
the cluster of dark-gold bodies, we hesitated,

then reached for the soft electric
mass. Their hum broadcast
through our fingertips, our
hands vanished—they let us in.

Dreaming Seasons

Pipeline hearings have begun
in Kitamaat. All the wild animals,
insects, even mycelium absorb
the real-time sound: construction
worms west. A slow, precise greed
with its own private police force
pushes toward the ocean,
the open market. I step out
of the liquor store holding vodka
by the neck, a wolf howls
from somewhere in the mountains
that loom over a section of
highway locals call "Misery Mile"
—still coated in hoar frost. An
abandoned car remains on its side
in the ditch where the road bends.
You should drive slowly around
the lake. Someone said this one is
fathomless. Do we even know its
true name? Fuel light comes on,
and over the prairies a freak
warm wind talks sparse trees into
somnambulance. They can't even
tell if they're dreaming anymore.
In their panic, they begin to bud.

Salmon Berries

I eat them ready or not;
sweet or electric sour
races along my tongue,

through my cheek, jawbone.
A bird shadow flashes
across the crisp expanse

of golden lawn. Like your
absence, which just passed
through me again.

Ferry

Last sailing, scattered,
subdued passengers.

In the deep, blue slip
of twilight, windows

reflect their interior; we're
now translucent amusement

park ghosts. Commuting home,
we glide past another ferry,

lit up, revealing figurines
(so we must be to them).

They speed by—
time-lapse, then they're

gone. We return to
the illusion of stillness.

*

All over the world scientists
monitor rising ocean acidity,

count microplastics, track
real-time electronic signals

from tags fastened to
migrating animals. Before

each failed pregnancy came
a faithful dream of being under

water—in an ocean. In these dreams
I can breathe, but keep forgetting

where you are. In the seventh pregnancy,
the dream changes: I dive under water,

but this time it's a swimming pool,
I can see the tiled bottom. Resting there

is an opalescent egg within reach.
What am I supposed to do?

Someone tells me *When the guava turn
pink, the river will be full of salmon.*

*

My father hangs out at the periphery
of my dream. I know he's dead and

cannot stay. I'm looking through
boxes he left. In one, brittle handbound

books, in another, quartz crystals:
palm-sized, honey-coloured.

This morning the crossing
is rocky. We are heaved side

to side. The vessel's salt-spittled
windows tilt between a dark

metal sea, nicked with whitecaps,
and a concrete sky. It suddenly came back

to me—that October morning my father
recounted his morphine-fueled dream:

It is the 1800s, in an alpine cabin
full of strangers. On his arm, a tattoo

of a paratrooper. He sees another
man with the same tattoo, whispers

Hey, you're from the future, like me.
The man looks over everyone

in that cabin, slowly turns back to him.
We all are.

Fortune Teller Miracle Fish

My father taught me to fish
when I was seven. How to
bait the hook, the motion of
arm through to wrist. I learned
to lift my finger from the line
at the right moment, send
hook and float sailing

in an arc, with the buzzing hum
of line unspooling. When I
was grown and away, he would
buy a retirement home, wetland
adjacent, ringed by cedars, fir,
hemlock, alder, orange-gold
arbutus in calligraphic

twists against cerulean sky,
fluorescent-green mosses,
bone-white deer lichen. If I return
my father's ashes to the land
he once owned, do I now believe
he belongs to the earth?

As a child in Chinatown, I bought
a Fortune Teller Miracle Fish.
Small, red cellophane, sleeved
in thin, white plastic. Placed
in the palm, the fish begins to move,
curls in on itself, reveals our
true nature. Or at least what

we're thinking. I was nine when I first
fished alone, casting off a worn,
sun-warmed dock. The line grew
taught, I began to reel it in,
like anyone young about to
open a gift. A fish the size of my
palm writhed on the hot, silvered

planks. Suddenly a baby fish slipped
from the iridescent belly, glossed in
a scant film of blood. My hands
hurried to free the hook from
the mother's lip, gather their
faltering bodies, drop them back
into the necessary ocean, leaning

over the edge of dock, *I'm sorry
I'm sorry I'm sorry.* Trying
to see if they'd make it. Slip
of time, future, step, fortune, girl.
When we say *body of water,*
do we believe it is contained?

Acknowledgements

I am grateful for the financial support from the Canada Council of the Arts and from Arts NL in the making of this book.

Several of these poems or previous versions have appeared in the Canadian publications *Riddle Fence*, *Arc*, *Vallum*, *Room*, *Prairie Fire*, and *CV2*. Much thanks to these editors and all who keep literary magazines afloat.

A huge and heartfelt thanks to the incredibly skilled team at Riddle Fence Publishing for their dedication to making literary space for debut authors, for taking a chance on my manuscript, and ushering my first book into the world.

So much respect and gratitude to my editor Adèle Barclay for their insight and instinct in helping fine-tune and shape this manuscript into its final form.

This book had a long gestation. Over its more than fifteen years of becoming, I've had many teachers and mentors who've encouraged and given me wayfinding tools in the poetic wilderness. Deepest thanks to Evelyn Lau, Jami Macarty, Patrick Lane, the 2008 Banff Writing Studio with Don McKay, John Steffler, Mary Dalton, my MFA teachers at UBC Okanagan—Nancy Holmes and Sharon Thesen—The Quebec Writers' Federation and poetry mentor Peter Richardson, and Hoa Nguyen. At a point when I was doubtful of this project, I participated in the Writers NL mentorship program with poet Mark Callanan. His feedback helped reignite faith in my own words—thank you. And a big shout-out to Writers NL for all that they do for the NL literary community. Grateful for the feedback from writers in residence: Jordan Scott (SFU), George Murray (Memorial University) and Leah Horlick (University of Calgary).

During my time in St. John's, Ktaqmkuk, I felt unbelievably lucky to have found myself in a talented, thoughtful poetry group. For their friendship, feedback, and snacks, much gratitude to Maggie Burton, Matthew Hollett, Anna Swanson, and Don McKay (who mostly hosted us).

Big love and thanks to friends and kin who've provided unwavering support, who have read and reflected on many early versions of these poems. Jen Charles, Nicole Crouch, Tamara Kater, Clea Minaker, Rebekah Robbins, Erin Senior, and Anna Swanson. My immediate and extended family—especially my late grandma Helen who encouraged my love of reading, writing, and creating, and my mom Roberta Meilleur, and dad Robbie McLennan, who always nurtured my creativity and predilection for the less-travelled path. There's not enough room here to name and thank everyone I'd like to, but please know my gratitude extends to you.

Love and profound appreciation to my partner Peter Yang for always being an anchor through the highs and lows and helping me make time to fit the writing in. Unending love and thanks to my son Coen for teaching me, for making me a mother.

Tia McLennan's (she/her) poetry has appeared in various Canadian literary journals including *Riddle Fence*, *Vallum*, *Arc*, *CV2*, *Room*, and *Prairie Fire*. In 2022, she won the NLCU Fresh Fish Award for her unpublished poetry manuscript. She holds an interdisciplinary MFA in creative writing and visual art from UBC Okanagan, and a BFA from Nova Scotia College of Art and Design University. Originally from so-called Vancouver Island, B.C., (territory of the K'ómoks people), she now gratefully resides in kalpilin (Pender Harbour), B.C. with her partner, their five-year-old son and their very large grey and white gentleman cat named Basho.